T0413972

TOM REYNOLDS

GET OFF
YOUR PHONE
AND
START LIVING

A Guide to Lifelong Connections, Friendships and Personal Fulfillment

DEDICATION

I would like to dedicate this book to the two most wonderful women in my life:

To my daughter Meg, who is a fantastic, fun and very respectful young lady who fills me with pride day in and day out. Every time I see her or hear her voice it warms my heart.

To my love Ann, who is my shining armor, my love and my best friend and partner forever and ever.

"To bring about change, you must not be afraid to take the first step."

—Rosa Parks

"We need not wait to see what others do."

—Mahatma Gandhi

"Count your age by friends, not years. Count your life by smiles, not tears."

—John Lennon

TABLE OF CONTENTS

PREFACE

I have never written a book before for the simple reason that, up until now, I did not think I had anything of real value to share with readers. I do not think I am creative enough to put together a great book of fiction with terrific characters and plenty of plot twists. Nor, having spent over thirty-five years in marketing and sales roles for a huge food and beverage company, did I believe that I had any real important wisdom to impart if I wrote a nonfiction or a self-help book.

That has changed due to the invention of the smartphone.

Cell phones, as we know them today, are indeed the most productive tool ever invented. But they are also the most nonproductive product device ever invented because they are driving us apart.

My observations over the past ten years are that cell phones (laptops and tablets as well) can connect people around the world but they are also driving loneliness and self-esteem issues, and prohibiting people from talking to one another in meaningful ways.

This book is not a self-help, ten-step program to stop your screen addiction. There are many terrific books on the market that will help with that.

What this book is meant to do is to provide you with an alternative to cell phone obsession. That is, to help you see that lifelong connections, friendships and acquaintances will be far more fulfilling than where most people are today.

So, let's get started ...

THE PROBLEM

According to the United Nations, the average human life expectancy in the United States in 2024 is 79 years of age. Multiple recent studies indicate that the average United States resident is projected to spend between 17 to 18 years online over their lifetime.

Yes, an estimated 21 percent of our lifetimes will be spent in a digital existence, not in the real world. Think about that for a minute.

There is an alternative to this obsession people have with their cell phones, laptops, tablets and game consoles.

I will try to point out ten to 12 day-to-day situations, locations and circumstances where you can and should put down your cell phone and engage with those around you.

I will try to use my own observations and experiences as much as I can, but I will also include societal research to hammer some points home.

So, give it a read and please give it a chance because you will hopefully see that there is more to life than playing with your cell phones.

PHONE UBIQUITY AND APPS

Smartphones are everywhere in the world. At the end of 2023, there were 6.9 billion smartphones worldwide which means 86 percent of this planet's population has a smartphone. The numbers are higher if you add basic cell phones to the mix.

There is no doubt that smartphones are indeed one of the best inventions ever created. They allow us to:

- Call friends from anywhere to anywhere
  even nutty Aunt Betty
- Buy thousands of goods and services
  that you cannot afford
- Order an Uber ride after a late night out
- Check sports scores to see if you won the bet
- Make plane and hotel reservations to exotic locales
- Take thousands of useless photos
- Make appointments and check personal calendars
- Use GPS so that us knuckleheads don't get lost
- To connect with the world on social media

The first smartphone was introduced in 2007 by Apple Inc. Subsequent updates and competitors have flocked the market ever since. This handheld computer is truly the most remarkable productivity tool ever created.

For those of you over the age of 35 or so, do you remember having to use a house phone to make telephone calls, look up numbers in the phone book, buy maps at the convenience store to get to Uncle Jerry's house five hours away for Thanksgiving, go see or call a travel agent to make flight reservations or carry around a ten-pound camera to take pictures?

Yes, the smartphone has indeed really changed our lives and made them a heck of a lot more productive.

However, these smartphones have also not only made our lives less productive, they have *also* led us to be more distracted, lacking in self-esteem, more isolated, seriously lacking in basic social skills and lessened our ability to interact with those around us.

The basic problem is cell phone obsession and even cell phone addiction for some.

A few facts to consider: the average American spends five hours a day on their cell phone. That is roughly 21 percent of every single day. (See Notes and References at the end of the book for data sources.)

If you assume you will use a cell phone for sixty years, it adds up to over 109,000 hours over your "phone-using lifetime". For those of you who like math, the numbers are as follows:

- Five hours a day equals 1,825 hours per year
- If you use a cell phone from when you are ten years old until you are 70 years old, it equals 109,500 hours

- Total hours over 60 years (24 hours x 365 days x 60 years) equals 525,600 hours you have to spend on Earth

The numbers are much higher for Millennials and Gen X'ers, which is over six hours a day or 25 percent of every day. Over their lifetime, it adds up to 131,400 hours of cell phone time (trust me, I did the math).

At the extreme, 13 percent of Millennials and five percent of Boomers spend 12 hours a day on their cell phones.

Spending six-plus hours daily on the phone would be one thing if people were talking to loved ones on their devices; however, people are not doing that, they are spending six-plus hours daily on social media.

Social media is a huge problem.

On average, Americans spend 64 minutes a day on Facebook and 48 minutes a day on Instagram. YouTube remains the most popular platform for teens, over 90 percent use the site and over 20 percent use it constantly.

These social media apps are designed to promote and encourage connectivity with friends, classmates and family – which they certainly do.

However, they are also designed by Big Tech to become addictive.

It is no big secret that large social media companies like Twitter/X, Facebook, Instagram, TikTok and YouTube make billions of dollars in revenues and profits per year. How do they do this when the platforms are free? Simply put, advertising.

Advertisers want eyeballs on the goods and services they sell. What better way to advertise than on social media platforms that are very addictive? It has been proven by many studies and comments from former Big Tech employees that the sites are intended to do just that.

I will not get into all the science mumbo jumbo about how these social media platforms were designed to manipulate us by activating chemicals in our brain, specifically dopamine. Suffice it to say, if a social media session fuels the release of dopamine, it is something that we want to experience time and time again; so we do in spades.

These social media platforms ostensibly were created to promote connectivity with friends and family, and they certainly do provide that feature.

Humans are social creatures; they want to connect, but there are significant downsides to the "connectivity." For example, say you are twenty years old, and you and your college friends post spring break vacation photos. In your case, you get virtually no "likes" on Facebook or Instagram but your other college friends get close to 100 "likes." Today that is the equivalent of public humiliation, which can lead to anxiety, loneliness and even, in some cases, depression.

This is one of the reasons that in a recent survey, 79 percent of 18 to 24-year-olds felt lonely, compared to only 40 percent of those over sixty-six years old.

Another big downside of social media and general phone obsession is the "fear of missing out." Why do you think the average American picks up their cell phone over 50 times a day and for 18 to 24-year-olds, it is over 90 times a day? It is this general anxiety that people have, especially younger ones, that they are not in the loop, have missed a party, or did not like or respond to a photo quickly enough.

Don't people find this exhausting?

Yes, they certainly do! People are more tired, distracted, depressed and lonelier than ever before. It was true pre-Covid, but it is only getting worse post-Covid.

This all leads me to the basic principle of this book, which is smartphone obsession has led to most people having little to no basic social skills. Most folks spend significantly more time each and every day on their cell phones, laptops, tablets and game consoles than talking to classmates, friends, and family members. It is not exactly a degradation of society that historically was filled with deep one-on-one connections or fulfilling group connections, but it is getting pretty close.

So, with that said, in the following chapters I would like to point out ten to 12 situations, locations and circumstances where we can or should put down our smartphones and start engaging with those around us.

SPORTING EVENTS AND CONCERTS

I have been going to professional and collegiate sporting events for the last fifty-five years or so (yes, I am that old). I love the competition, the strategy, the crowd and the ability now to make a bit of a bet on the outcome of the games.

I was very, very fortunate to have worked for The Gatorade Company for almost 35 years in the United States and in Europe. Through that association, I attended Super Bowls, World Series, World Cups and many other phenomenal sporting events. I was able to share those experiences with work colleagues, family and friends.

One of the many reasons I enjoy live sporting events is the ability to come together as a college or city community and root for the home team. While attending games, it is great to talk to those sitting around you about your particular team and share stories. In fact, I became lifelong friends with a few people who I first met at games, especially at the New York Giants football games.

Nowadays, it is really hard to even speak to those sitting around you because, you guessed it, they are constantly on their phones.

I recently flew to Houston to attend a Houston Texans versus Cleveland Browns football playoff game with my daughter, Meg, and her boyfriend, Jake. I was shocked at how many people missed so many of the great plays in the game because they were doing you know what.

Why do people pay hundreds of dollars apiece for tickets, parking, food and such to spend an inordinate amount of their time at the game playing with their phones? They are taking dozens of photos, texting constantly with people who are not at the game, posting pictures on social media, etc., etc. Are they trying to tell the world they are at the game? Who wants to see fifteen photos of you at a playoff game when they are at home, in say Cleveland, and have been shoveling snow for the past hour and a half? And, to boot, these people at the Houston Texans game were mostly grown-ass adults.

An even more extreme case this past summer was the Taylor Swift Eras Concert Tour craze. If you were able to get tickets, and that was a big if, the average *face value* cost per ticket was $499, plus the exorbitant fees. If you were like most people and paid for them on the secondary market, the average cost per ticket was $1,620, plus the lovely fees.

According to my nieces Carly, Ellie, Zoe and Maddie, the concert was super awesome and they had a blast. I'm not sure their parents thought it was so cool when they got their credit card bills a month later, but I digress.

Every news clip and published picture I saw last summer during Taylor Swift's Eras Concert Tour had one thing in common – people with their phones in the air, taking videos and snapping pictures. And, guess what they did with the photos and videos? Yes, they would post pictures and send texts to their unfortunate "followers" who could not attend the concert. Why on Earth are you so mean to do that? Wouldn't it have been a better experience to put your phone away and sing, or better yet dance, with friends and strangers for a few hours? To talk and make some new friends?

I am very fortunate to be happily retired (said differently, unemployed) so I have a lot of free time on my hands. For the past six summers or so, we (my fantastic girlfriend Ann and I) have rented a beach house in Del Mar, California. Two of the reasons why we go there is the awesome weather and the Del Mar Thoroughbred Racetrack.

We absolutely love going to the racetrack in the summer. You get to handicap the races, have a few beers, make a few bets, "people-watch" the racetrack characters and basically chill out. It also helps that we own about 40 horses in a partnership group called "Eclipse Thoroughbred Partners," who do a phenomenal job.

Nowadays, there are many folks who attend the four-to-five-hour race day but never leave their seats. They can order food and beverages on their phone, handicap a race on their tablet and place a wager on said phone or tablet. That is option number one, which numerous people young and old do day in and day out at the Del Mar Thoroughbred Racetrack. Nothing terribly wrong with that approach.

We, on the other hand, have chosen option number two for the past few years, which is simply to walk around and talk to people. Jeez, we are forever grateful for choosing that routine.

Every day and every race, we go down to the paddock to see the horse's parade and get saddled, and we talk to people we know and do not know. After that, we go see a live teller like our friends, Bryan and Ronnie, and make a wager. The next step is to walk around the grandstand chatting away with folks, again those we know and do not know. Following that, we go to our box seats and watch the races and talk to all the other box seat holders around us, especially our box seat neighbors, Jeff and Milena.

11

Two different approaches and two different experiences.

We are so grateful that we take the "walk around approach." On an average day, we see about fifty people who we know by name and converse with or, at least, wave at. We now know the folks who work in valet parking, at the entrance gate, tellers, ushers, security people, trainers, grooms, and jockeys. We have also met a ton of folks who are patrons that come from around the country, like our great friend Jim who we met at the track, others who live in Southern California, others who own local restaurants, like our dear friend Maurizio, or are simply racing fans.

So, in closing out this chapter, I would like you to consider "the walk around and say hello" approach at sporting events and concerts instead of spending so much time on your phone "conversing and posting" with people far away instead of with those around you.

OFFICE BUILDINGS AND APARTMENTS

After I retired, we decided to sell the suburban home I owned near my office and move to an apartment in a wonderful building in downtown Dallas. Frankly, I wanted to simplify my life and not have to worry about paying for broken air-conditioning units, old refrigerators, washers and dryers going kaput, and all of the other expensive upkeep that goes with owning a home.

We moved to a lovely apartment building close to a long running/biking trail and within walking distance of numerous bars and restaurants. The building has fantastic amenities, including a large pool, two fitness centers, barbecue grills, a business center, a coffee station and the like. The apartment complex caters to mostly young folks that are primarily 22 to 35 years old, which is great with us since "the young ones keep us old ones young." In a nutshell, after ten years of living in the same apartment in the same building, we can unequivocally say that we love it.

However, making new friends in the apartment building has not been that easy. I can certainly understand why a fair amount of

22- to 35-year-olds do not want to hang out with a 66-year-old (me) or maybe a 54-year-old (Ann). However, it is not just the age thing, because the 22 to 35-year-olds hardly even talk to each other. Almost never.

For the life of me, I cannot understand why, when neighbors walk in the hallways, enter an elevator, or work out at the building's gym, they cannot look up from their phones and, at least, say "good morning" or "hello." Worse yet, in the summer months, people are at the pool sitting on chaise lounges four feet away from each other for one to three hours and never acknowledge that you even exist – like you are an inanimate figure or a blow-up doll, for goodness' sake.

Having said all that, we have been extremely fortunate to have made some very dear (and very young) friends in the building that we socialize with quite a bit. The way we met and connected was simply in the gym, in an elevator or most likely we just started up a conversation at the pool. The common denominator was that we were not obsessed with our phones when we met. For that reason, a toast to our fantastic neighbors in the building who we eat, drink, and sometimes travel with:

Anthony	Kaylee and Cade	Tanner
Bobby and Cassie	Ryan	Carl
Connor	Brian and Annie	Lauren
Nick	Ethan	
Audrey	Ashley	

On another note, I noticed that in this day and age, it has been hard for people to make friends, even in the office buildings where they work three to five days a week. You are probably thinking I am going to blame phone obsession on this, but I am not. The culprit here is not smartphones, but laptops and tablets.

When I was working 50-plus hours a week, either in the office or traveling around the country, I spent way too much time on my laptop responding to 150-plus emails each day, in addition to writing sales presentations, approving budgets and the like. After my first year working at Frito-Lay, Inc.'s headquarters in Texas, I realized that I hardly knew anyone outside of my work group of about 30-to-40 people, and our office had over 2,000 employees working in the building!

Instead of being cooped up all day in my office or just walking around our small work area, I decided that I needed to get out of our confined space and "wander around." I did not sit in the cafeteria for hours bothering people who had work to do, and I did not just walk around to random people's cubicles and start up a conversation. That, putting it mildly, would be big-time creepy and annoying.

What I did instead was, for 30 minutes a day, start responding to emails and phone calls from outside our small work group in person. At first, it was a bit awkward for me and some individuals that I visited but, as time passed, it worked out exceptionally well.

Think about it for a moment: work colleagues contacted me by email or left me a voicemail message for a response. Returning with an answer in person made them feel cared for and important. By the end of the year's experiment, I knew so many more people in the building, which was my original intent. An added bonus was that it helped the business I was running become more efficient and successful. Most importantly, some of those people I met while I was "wandering around" have been friends to this day, and this happened almost twenty years ago.

I know these days that many, many people work at home in a virtual environment so it is much harder to make deep, personal connections with colleagues than it is if you were at the office four to five days a week. However, with a bit of effort, you can overcome that obstacle. Let me give you a real-life example from my career.

My first big boy job out of college 44 years ago was as a marketing assistant with the Quaker Oats Company. One of my responsibilities was to forecast canned dog food sales for every item and package size we sold nationally. Then I broke that forecast down to the ten warehouses scattered across the country. If I did my job correctly, we would always have every item in stock when a customer ordered it anywhere in the United States.

A big part of my data analysis hinged on getting input from the eight sales regions on a monthly basis. Since I did not have the budget to travel to each sales region's offices, most of this was done by phone (we did not have office computers then). I literally had a two-foot by three-foot piece of paper where I would write out the forecast by hand with warehouse locations across the top and items on the left axis. As the newbie in the department, I got all the crappy grunt work for sure (and should have).

What does this have to do with making great personal connections with colleagues in a virtual working world?

I believe that working from home today poses the same issues as it did for me 40-plus years ago. The issue then, was the sales regions were doing over 30 different brand forecasts every month. Were they spending any real, quality time on mine? Could I assume they were somewhat accurate? Remember, I only talked to them by phone so we had not built up any meaningful personal connection.

What I did was, when the eight sales managers came into our head-quarters location from time to time, I would always try to have lunch and/or dinner with them. I continued doing this for years and years, which then developed into some terrific and meaningful personal connections. Especially so with our Denver Region Sales Manager, Dave.

Fast forward ten years later when I was starting up the Gatorade business in Europe. In a nutshell, I did a really crappy job and was told I would be fired in the next two months. As I was preparing to move back to the United States and look for a job, I received a phone call from the aforementioned Dave who was by then the Head of Sales for Gatorade in the United States. Blowing me away, he offered me a job to be the Gatorade Director of Sales for the newly created position on the West Coast.

After stammering for a while, I asked him if he asked my boss and his boss (who was going to fire me) if this was okay and he said: "Yes, I went to bat for you and they acquiesced."

Thankfully, I did not let him down and we crushed our sales numbers for many years in a row after that.

The moral of the story, in my opinion, is that you can never have enough meaningful personal friendships at work. You just have to try to make them in a creative way.

I believe making these deep connections by phone or on Zoom calls is nearly impossible. Yet, there are many options if you are working from home. Some of them include:

- Inviting your colleagues to lunch
- Having a dinner party at your home or at a restaurant
- Starting a book club or football pool with coworkers
- Driving or even flying on your own dime to your company headquarters

So, if you are working at an office try returning calls and/or emails in person and, if you are working virtually, get a bit creative and try to figure out how to make some terrific personal connections with your colleagues.

RESTAURANTS

This chapter has the potential to be one of my favorites and the one I talk the most about when describing phone obsession.

Let's begin with some data on why people eat away from home. According to many surveys, the most important reasons why people dine out are as follows:

- The biggest reason – 75 percent of those surveyed – was that they did not want to cook. Since cooking entails knowing how to cook, planning a menu, shopping for ingredients, actually cooking, and finally dealing with the sloppy and messy cleanup afterwards.
- Many other people state that they eat away from home because it is convenient for them (54 percent of those surveyed).
- Others (48 percent) mention that they enjoy the socialization, camaraderie and relaxation while dining out.
- Still others (38 percent) mention that they like to have unlimited choices in the types of restaurants, the choices offered and the ability to try different and new cuisines while they are out.

- Although many people will not mention this in surveys, a big reason they like to eat away from home is because they are simply lazy.

Given all these reasons, especially the third one, that almost 50 percent of those surveyed stated that they want to socialize and relax while dining out, why are folks on their phones all the time at every restaurant across America? It is true at sandwich shops, fast food places, bars, casual restaurants, and medium to very high-end fine dining establishments. Think about a few eating-out scenarios or occasions where this plays out and is, quite frankly, somewhat asinine.

Let's start with a family's night out. Imagine two parents with their two to three children, ages six through 12, dining out at a fairly nice restaurant. Now granted, I am a bit over-observant about this topic, but it is bewildering to me when I frequently see a family out to dinner and all of them are individually on some type of electronic device. Mom and Dad on their cell phones and all the kids are playing some sort of game on their tablets.

Why did they even leave the house? They could have done those same darn things at home (at least without the cooking part). But, if that is the way dinner is going to be, why not order takeout or Uber Eats? I know I am old, but dinner out as a young child was an amazing special treat for the Reynolds household. Besides that, dinner away from home was another way for the whole family to interact, talk, ask questions of each other, and find out what was going on at school and at work. It simply mystifies me when I see what happens during "family night" out nowadays.

Now, let's chat about date night out. I will make this paragraph short and sweet. If one or both of the people on the date are on their phone semi-frequently, the relationship is sour and likely doomed. Here is a very strong suggestion: if you are going out on a date night, take only one phone out with you. My fantastic girlfriend, Ann, has never once, in at least 250 date nights over the past five-plus years, taken her phone out with her. The only reason I take my phone is so we can get an Uber or Lyft ride to and from the restaurant (and that way I get to pay for the rides back and forth. Thanks, sweet Ann!). Please take only one phone. Try it sometime. It may be hard at first, but the conversation, camaraderie and intimacy will make it a special night out.

If the phone thing happens on a *first* date, which actually did happen to me six or seven years ago (she started with the phone playing), you should not make it past the cocktail and salad portions of that first and last encounter. Enough said.

If you are having a night out with friends, please put your phones away for at least an hour or more. I understand that people want to take and share pictures and show goofy cat videos that they think are funny. But, for the love of God, the reason you are all out together having drinks and dinner is to socialize, interact, get to know one another better and bond further. Getting on Instagram, X or TikTok while people are trying to converse with you and enjoy a meal is simply rude. Someone needs to take the initiative to "put the phones away" for the next hour; why can't it be you?

Finally, since we are chatting about restaurants, I thought I would impart a little-known fact that may surprise you: many medium to high-end restaurants are watching and taking notes on your behaviors while dining.

If you frequent some nice restaurants, many of the managers and staff have cliff notes on what you are like, what your preferences are, your habits while dining and whether you are high maintenance or not. The reason some restaurants keep notes is because they want to serve you better once they get to know you a bit (or do not want to serve you better if you and your mates are jerks).

The way it used to work was that the waiter, waitress, or manager would write a list of your personal preferences on a piece of paper, such as dietary restrictions, slow or fast diners, favorite waiter, what section of the restaurant you like, food and wine preferences and many other specifics to make your visit more enjoyable. Today, with phone apps such as Open Table and Resy, the restaurant management team can simply input those specific preferences directly into their reservation system.

On the day or night of your reservation, the restaurant team will print or handwrite your "card" and give it to your waitress once you arrive. The reason I bring this up is that you want to be comfortable with what is written on that "card". From our experience (there are about ten to twelve restaurants in Dallas that have cards on Ann and I), the cards are fairly accurate but you never know. You can simply ask the waitstaff if they have a "card" on you and politely ask them what is written on your card (occasionally the waitstaff will leave the card on your table by mistake, so you can just read it yourself).

By getting to know many restauranteurs in Dallas, Texas, and Del Mar, California, I have seen some rather bizarre comment cards on people we do not know which is why I included this topic. The common denominator on negative comment cards, besides people just being nasty or rude, is the phone thing.

The following is an example of someone's comment card that was stealthily shared with me by the owner of a steakhouse in Dallas:

- Overall, a bit difficult at times
- Always on the phone
- Even uses FaceTime at the table against our policy
- Normally orders the specials
- Low tippers

Do you want that to be your restaurant comment card?

Another little tidbit about restaurants that you may plan to frequent often, is that you should try to get the owner's or the manager's cell phone number. It may seem a bit odd to you that they may provide it readily, but they are usually delighted that you want to come back often. In my experience, they will provide their cell phone number 90 percent of the time (I have fifteen-plus of them listed in my contacts).

If your request fails the first time, try again or ask for the chef to come to your table after dinner and compliment them on the meal or ask the owner or General Manager to come over and do the same with them. Once you get their cell phone numbers, you can almost always get a reservation even on very busy nights, and they, the General Manager or the owner, will know you are coming and will frequently stop by to say hello and make sure everything is to your liking.

So, to close out this chapter, please go out and enjoy meals with your friends, family and loved ones. Either leave the phones and tablets behind or, at least, minimize the use of them for the one to two hours you are at the restaurant. The purpose of going out to eat is to socialize, learn more about each other, laugh, tell stories, be goofy and relax.

AIRPORTS
AND AIRLINES

I have been very fortunate to have traveled extensively for work and pleasure over the past 45 years. Within my working life of 35 years, I have been to almost every major city in the United States and Western Europe. Over almost a half-century time span, I have accumulated over five million miles on American Airlines and continue to accumulate 100,000 to 150,000 additional miles each year in retirement. Suffice it to say, that I have seen many things in airports and hotels while traveling.

For kicks and grins, I will walk you through a sequence of phone obsession events I frequently see while I am traveling.

Let's start with what I see at the airport. For most people, airline travel is stressful and quite overwhelming. Individuals are worried about being on time, getting bags checked, going through security and probably stopping to get some food and beverages for the flight.

Then why, from my viewpoint, do people make it harder and more harried for themselves by being on their phones instead of focusing

on the task at hand – which is getting through the airport success-
fully and on time?

It seems like every fifth passenger going through TSA security is
unprepared and does NOT have their boarding pass or identification
ready for inspection. It is not because they are chatting with their
friends or family who are with them. It is because they are texting,
reading emails, responding to emails or on social media looking at
other peoples' darn business or vacation trips. What the heck people;
get your act together, be nice to the TSA agents and get through the
line quickly.

Once people have cleared the security hurdle, it is time for the mad-
house zoo adventure, which is commonly known as a terminal con-
course. This is where the real fun begins!

People are trying to figure out where their gate is, where the bathroom is located and possibly looking for the food court. Somehow,
they cannot find any of them because they are either looking at their
screens or have, in some bizarre way, forgotten how to read signs.

I see this each day in every airline terminal I have visited in the past
ten years or more.

By way of background, I do volunteer a few shifts a month at the
Dallas-Fort Worth International Airport (DFW) Information Desk.
Think about me as a Wal-Mart greeter: "Hi, may I help you?" is basi-
cally the role.

I get to see this train wreck of watching people unsuccessfully navi-
gate the terminal in a quick and efficient manner for four to six hours
a month. I have seen people on their phones: trip over other people's
suitcases, trip over their own suitcases (very bad form and highly
embarrassing), run into the golf carts transporting the elderly, run
head first into other people, fall into rope lines by the gates, etc., etc.

Consequently, individuals who are *that* distracted by their prized cell phones are obviously problematic and a bit dangerous. For the life of me, I cannot figure out why, when people do put their phones away for a few precious minutes, they all of a sudden forget how to read.

My girlfriend Ann (who is a flight attendant) and I experience distracted people all the time in airports. We could be standing ten yards away from a bathroom and people ask us "Where is the bathroom?". Literally, there is a sign behind us that is two feet tall, in English and with male/female pictograms and you are asking us where the restroom is? What happened to you?

Another wonderful example is elevators. I will use the DFW airport as an example, but it happens all the time at many airports around the country. At the DFW airport, curbside baggage check and ground transportation are downstairs and airline check-in, security, departures and baggage claim are upstairs. To be clear, there are only two levels.

A dozen or more times this past year someone has gotten on the elevator and asked me/us what floor should they push. WHAT? If you are getting on the elevator, you are obviously taking a ride up one level or down one level. There are no other choices people. Moreover, there are signs that you could read in ten seconds that say, for example, "departures" or "ground transportation" right next to the only two buttons. When did people forget how to read? Okay, enough of that off-topic diatribe.

On a recent DFW airport shift during the March Spring Break rush of 2024, I was able to clearly see what the benefits could be of me *not* being on my phone.

As I began my two-and-one-half-hour shift, a pleasant young college student gave me a wallet he found in a nearby hallway. I called the DFW airport police to have them pick up the wallet so that they could take it to the lost and found kiosk in another terminal. About twenty minutes later, as I was sitting in the Information Booth, I overheard two TSA agents who were about 20 to 25 feet away chatting with a young gentleman, and they all seemed perplexed and confused. I walked over to them and asked if I could help. Well, sure enough, the young man was asking them where lost and found was because he had lost his wallet. I asked him his name and, of course, the wallet (that was still sitting in my back pocket) was his. The moral of the story is if I was scrolling around on my phone, I would never have overheard the group's conversation and the young lad would not have gotten his wallet back that night, especially since he had a connecting flight to catch to San Diego.

An hour later, I overheard another conversation between a mom and about six or seven older teenagers who were connecting planes in Dallas. She was advising the group that it was now 6:00pm and their flight was leaving at 7:40pm so they could walk around until 7:00pm and then meet at a specific gate. Because I was sure she was wrong, I glanced at my watch and confirmed that it was not almost 6:00pm in Dallas but it was around 7:00pm. Indeed, it was 7:00pm! Before all the kids scattered (and missed their flight), I walked over to the group to politely inform them of the time zone issue. The mother did not believe me at first because she kept looking at her watch but once she dragged her phone out of her humongous purse, she realized I was right. Thankfully they rushed and made their flight which was wonderful, but it likely would not have happened if I was playing on my phone and did not overhear their conversation.

Getting back on topic, let's talk about boarding an aircraft and settling in on the flight.

Most airlines have a boarding process that goes by groups (1-8 or A, B, C). On paper, this seems like a good idea in order to avoid 200-plus people crowding the jet bridge entryway all at once. Unfortunately, it seems that 200-plus people cannot follow simple instructions by the gate agents because, instead of paying attention, they are on their phones texting or playing games. The thirty-to-forty people in groups one and two have to bump and shove their way forward in order to get near the jet bridge because the other 160-170 people in groups three through eight are in their way playing with their phones.

Once individuals are on the airplane, it gets even more infuriating! I am not sure when it became socially acceptable to talk on the phone (or worse yet have speakerphone turned on) while you are seated on a plane. I get why it may be essential if it is some sort of emergency, but in my experience, 99 percent of the calls I overhear are about banal, silly topics and are pretty much about nothing of any importance.

Finally, the worst thing I continually experience once in the air is people watching and listening to movies, podcasts or television shows *without headphones.* Not only is this against Federal Aviation Administration (FAA) rules, it is simply rude and socially unacceptable. Think about it: if you are trying to read a book, take a nap or talk to your traveling companion, do you want to hear someone else's loud inappropriate movie? Heck no! I cannot tell you how many times it happens and, to make it worse sometimes, a few apprehensive flight attendants do not even enforce their own airline's policy, never mind the FAA's.

So, when traveling by plane, try to leave your phone in your carry-on bag while traversing the airport. There is no need to add to the stress of travel by trying to multitask through check-in, TSA security, navigating the airport and the like. Enjoy the business trip or the vacation and have some fun at the airport and on the plane with those around you.

FAMILY GATHERINGS, VACATIONS, AND CRUISES

Vacations with family and friends should be all about togetherness, catching up, fun and relaxation. Then why is it that I often see families, friends and vacation partners so stressed out while they are away from home?

The one obvious reason is that some people just do not know how to relax and enjoy a little bit of downtime. They either cannot sit still or are worried that they are missing something at home or at work. Those folks just need to grab a cocktail or a few glasses of wine and find a quaint quiet place to look at the view, read a book or take a nap.

Still, others continue to be stressed out or mentally far away from their annual vacation because they cannot put down their phones and keep them out of reach. These folks are constantly checking their work emails and voicemail messages, taking random photos, going on social media and the like. What the heck people! You are supposed to be on a fantastic trip with family and friends, and instead, you are checking on what other people are doing and not truly enjoying yourselves in the moment.

Recently, at a lovely all-inclusive Mexican Caribbean resort, I saw a family of about eighteen people checking in to the resort. I knew they were all together as a group because all of them were wearing the same cheesy T-shirts with the family name "Donahue" in full display on each. Two grandparents, eight adults and eight children aged from around six to 15 years old, all seemed so happy and all were in awe of the fabulous resort property.

Fast forward to the next day. I saw all of them (most were again wearing the goofy family reunion T-shirts) at the pool and/or at the beach. The strangest thing I noticed was that almost all of them, either frolicking in the ocean or swimming in the pool, were on their phones. The adults and kids were all a million miles away mentally from interacting with each other. This went on for hours and hours. The saddest part was that the two grandparents who were sitting under an umbrella – and were not on their phones – not only looked totally bored but were probably wondering why not one of the sixteen other family members would be having a conversation with them. I am sure they were thinking: "You came all this way and you spend your entire vacation time on an electronic device?".

Now, let's discuss college spring break. A great opportunity, if you can afford it, to blow off some steam and enjoy a fun trip with your buddies. Once again, why the phone obsession when you are supposed to be soaking up some rays, flying down the ski slopes, having a few too many adult beverages and enjoying each other's company?

I cannot fathom how many tens of millions of photos are posted on TikTok, X or Instagram every spring break season, but it is certainly a huge number. I mean, just from my thirteen nieces and nephews,

I see hundreds myself. Ask yourself how much time and effort went into posting those pictures. My sense is a ton of time. Think about it; for every picture "posted" how many were taken and then discarded as not good enough (be honest ladies)? My point is not to do this all day. It is not only taking away from the precious time you can converse and have fun with friends, but it can also come across as a bit rude and crass to those people back at home or in college who could not afford this awesome trip.

About one year ago, Ann and I went to Sydney, Australia (if you have never been, go there immediately; it is the most beautiful city these eyes have ever seen). We were enjoying having drinks on the bay near the Opera House when we saw a woman and her two-year-old toddler about twenty-five to thirty yards away from our table. She was mounting a tripod to take selfies of herself (not of her and her baby by the way). She proceeded to get so enamored with herself and her photos that she neglected to notice that her baby wandered away. Of course, Ann sprints and gets the baby, and I go over to the woman and not very politely tell her she may want to actually watch her child who is about ten yards away from the water. Ugh, what the heck is the matter with people who endanger an innocent child because of their phone addiction and narcissism?!

Finally, for this chapter, let's consider cruise vacations. I know some people love them and some people would not be caught dead on a cruise. For the record, my daughter Meg, Ann and I love them. It is great waking up almost every day in a different country or port, not having to frequently pack/re-pack, and the onboard meals and entertainment are terrific. Moreover, we have met some fabulous and fun people from all over the world on our many cruises.

For the life of me, I cannot figure out why people, while on the cruise ship, purchase the internet package so that they can continuously play on their phones while out to sea on the ship. First of all, at least on a Royal Caribbean cruise (which is fantastic by the way), the cost is $28 per person per day for internet service. For a family of four to purchase for a one-week trip, you will spend $784 for the internet package (trust me I did the math). That is the equivalent cost of a full year of internet service at home.

Why do people do it? The simple answer is phone obsession or addiction; pick your adjective.

One of the benefits of taking a cruise, for me, is that I can lock away my phone in the room safe for the whole week. Yes, the whole week! I am on vacation so I do not need the phone to check emails, return calls, catch up on social media, make dinner reservations or get an Uber or Lyft ride.

Recently a friend who I will call "G" went on a Caribbean cruise with his wife who he married a few years ago. Every day he posted pictures of beaches, meals or cocktails on our "boys' group" chat text thread. I finally asked him to either put the phone away in the safe and enjoy your awesome trip or stop texting us pictures of the warm lovely beaches of Aruba *when it's 25-30 degrees in Dallas and the wind is howling.*

So, folks when you gather the family for an awesome vacation, go on spring break, or take a cruise, please put the phones away for some part of each day or, in the case of a cruise, for the entire trip and enjoy each other's company.

DRIVING

This chapter should be the shortest and the most self-evident in this book. Unfortunately, it is not.

I assume if you ask 100 people if driving while using a phone to text or answer emails is dangerous, a minimum of ninety people would answer "yes." Furthermore, if you phrased the question "Do you think using your phone while driving is distracting?," then again I assume that at least ninety-nine people would say "yes".

Then why do so many people use a phone while driving, day in and day out?

The simple answer is that they are addicted to their phones, lazy, utterly selfish and have, in short, become irresponsible citizens.

A few statistics on this alarming trend:

- According to the National Safety Council, cell phone use while driving caused 1.6 million crashes in the United States in 2023.
- The same study shows that 660,000 people, at any given *hour* of the day, are attempting to use their phones while behind the wheel of an automobile.

- In 2022, there were 3,522 fatalities in the United States and over 362,000 injuries caused by our fellow citizens playing with their phones while driving. Preliminary data for the first nine months of 2023 imply that the 2022 numbers will, unfortunately, be far exceeded.
- The most inexperienced drivers (teenagers) admit that texting while driving is dangerous. 97 percent of teens agree that it is. Yet 48 percent of them admit to doing it anyway. It is no wonder that, according to the American Automobile Association (AAA), 16–17-year-old drivers are more likely to be involved in an accident that involved distracted driving.
- Car insurance rates have climbed enormously in the past few years since COVID due to more people on the road, higher car replacement costs and most importantly, an increase in accidents because more drivers are distracted.
- Finally, according to the National Highway Traffic Safety Administration, research suggests that texting while driving is far more dangerous than drunk driving.

This begs the question once again: why in the world are people being overly careless, dangerous, irresponsible and, quite frankly, negligent?

The answer is simple: phone obsession and addiction.

A quite pertinent and very alarming side anecdote that I witnessed three days ago while leaving downtown Dallas for the Dallas Fort Worth airport. I noticed a woman driving in front of me for about four to five miles. I observed at the first red light we approached that she had her phone mounted on her dashboard and was swiping at her phone often. By the second light we came to, it occurred to me that she was watching TikTok videos which is not too dangerous per se while stopped at a red light.

Once we got on a major highway at 65-70 MPH, she continued to swipe her phone every fifteen seconds or so. The entire time I was two to three car lengths behind her, she kept swiping her phone as she sped up, slowed down, moved over a foot into the right lane, then a few feet into the left lane, etc., etc. Needless to say, she was an accident waiting to happen, so I hit the gas and passed her to avoid being involved in a pileup at 70 MPH. I hope she made it home safely and enjoyed all the moronic videos she was watching. What a knucklehead !

Look, it takes a lot of effort to drive safely for the sake of yourself and others. It is a visually intensive sport.

You need to watch your speed, be cautious of tailgating, keep an eye out for two to three cars ahead of you, glance at the cars behind you and next to you, watch for turn signals, stop signs, yellow/red lights, stay clear of pedestrians crossing the roads (while on their phones), monitor brake light signals and the like. As I said, driving is and should be visually intense.

For goodness' sake, do not be a selfish, irresponsible, self-obsessed and generally negligent citizen – especially while driving.

So, for the love of your fellow Americans, stop texting, emailing, watching videos and catching up on Instagram or X while you are behind the wheel of a vehicle. Turn on the radio, catch up on some news, listen to a podcast or your favorite music instead. Or, better yet, just enjoy the ride and the view.

SOCIAL PLACES: PARKS, GYMS, BARS, MOVIES

A "social place" is a public space where people come together to interact and socialize. Examples include shopping malls, parks, pubs/bars, restaurants, gyms, community centers and the like.

The key word in the description above is that social places are locations where people come to *interact* with each other.

Then why is it that I hardly see any human interaction, or people talking to each other, in these so-called "social places"?

For example, yesterday I took an hour and a half walk on the Dallas Katy Trail that starts about 100 yards from our apartment. It is a beautiful trail with a great degree of tree covering, wide walkways, lovely flowers and tons of people.

For kicks and grins, I attempted to say good morning to everyone I passed along the four-to-five-mile roundtrip walk. In that hour-and-a-half time period, I got one "good morning" in return and a few nods of acknowledgment. That is no exaggeration whatsoever! One "good morning" from one person after passing over 100-120 people.

What was more important to them instead? Using their phones. They were either listening to music (frankly, which I was too) or talking on the phone, texting/reading emails, watching silly videos on TikTok or FaceTiming with someone. I get it that people are totally addicted and obsessed with their phones, but can't you at least take a moment to say good morning back to someone or at least acknowledge the greeting with a head nod?

As I mentioned in the Office Buildings and Apartments chapter, the residents in our apartment building are generally not very friendly or outgoing.

I happen to use the building's gym four to five times a week for an hour or so each day when I am in town. I always bring my iPod to listen to tunes but never my iPhone because I do not want to be interrupted by text messages, phone calls and other alerts from any damn app. In addition, probably no surprise to you since you have read this book almost all the way through, I like to verbally engage with people.

Well, guess what? I am not very successful at verbal engagement in our building's gym. I first start by waving hello or saying good morning to my fellow fitness enthusiasts and that usually gets me ignored or at best a nod. Absolutely no words of greeting are forthcoming my way.

Over time though, it works. I have made some very good friends being persistent, and I am very glad I did. The message is that even at the gym you can make some lifelong friends that share not only a desire to work out regularly but have other common interests as well.

Speaking of lifelong friends, here is an interesting "get off your phone and meet and interact with people story".

About ten Januarys ago, I moved to Dallas, Texas, from Plano, Texas, which is a suburb about twenty miles north of downtown Dallas. All my good buddies lived in or near Plano, and I did not know anyone well in Dallas. Frankly, it was time to meet some new friends.

As a starting point (besides the people in our apartment building, which was at the beginning quite an ordeal, as I have mentioned), I started going out on my own. It so happens that one of the highest-grossing bars/restaurants in all of Dallas called the Katy Trail Ice House was 100 feet away from my apartment. The place is fantastic, by the way, so if you are ever in Dallas, it is a must-visit for those who love a cold beer, a margarita and BBQ food. It also has a terrific outdoor patio.

A few times a week, I would wander over, sit at the bar and enjoy food and drinks for a few hours. My rule at the time was to never bring my phone to the Ice House so that I could meet people (although occasionally on slow nights I might have brought a book). Over time, I got to know about fifty-plus people that worked there and a bunch of us are still friends to this day. We have gone out to dinners together, attended pool parties and have been invited to a few weddings for some of the employees. Great fun.

In the first five months (February through June) of visiting the Katy Trail Ice House, I frequently saw three guys around my age sitting at the same table about thirty to fifty feet away from me and my barstool.

Fast forward to July of that same year, and I am sitting with friends in my box seats at the Del Mar Racetrack (as mentioned in Chapter 2), and I see three guys walk by in front of me who look familiar. I am thinking, thinking, thinking, "Where do I know these three dudes from?" When I see them walk by me again, it dawns on me that these are the same three guys that I have seen numerous times sitting at Table 53 at the Ice House.

I took the opportunity to follow them to their seats (Meg, this is not creepy sweetie), and I introduced myself to Ken, George and Harri and told them that I recognized them from the Ice House. At the end of the day, I invited them over to a dinner party we were having at my rental house in a few nights' time. They attended the dinner party and we had a blast together. A toast to ten years later, we are still good friends.

The moral of the story, as far as this book is concerned, is simple: if I spent all my time at the bar with my phone, I would have never seen them sitting at Table 53 that often. Nor would I have seen them at the racetrack if I was playing with my phone. Additionally, we would have likely never met and become lifelong friends.

Contrast my experience with the experience of a 25-year-old young lady I saw at the same bar this past Sunday night. I was standing at the bar when she walked up to order a drink while she was talking to someone on the phone with the speaker turned up all the way. The barkeep came over and asked her what she wanted to drink. The young lady (let's call her Karen) told her to hold on and pointed at her phone.

The bartender came back a minute or so later and asked her again for the drink order. Karen told her she was talking on the phone. The bartender came back again three to five minutes later and asked again, and Karen screamed at her for making her wait that long. To make a long story short, she caused such a silly obnoxious hissy fit that she never got a drink and was simply tossed from the establishment for being a Karen.

Understandably, if the phone call was an emergency and she was getting bad news about a health scare or something similar, I get it. In reality, the phone call with her girlfriend was about what they *might* do next weekend. Once again, do not walk into any retail establishment (nail salon, restaurant, store or bar) on your phone and expect any customer service at all because you simply do not deserve it, and it is rude to the employees and to those around you.

As a small side note, the Katy Trail Ice House has a policy that if you are walking, running or biking on the adjacent Katy Trail and are not a paying customer but need to simply use the restrooms, the hostesses and security personnel outside the bar ask that people leave their phones in a bucket while they use "the facilities". They do not want people saying they need to use the bathroom as a way to plop down at a table. A very simple, legitimate and appropriate request when there are tons of people waiting in line to enter the establishment.

To be clear, I do not have to tell you what kind of reaction that gets from some people. You would have thought that they were asking for a person's limb the way some people start becoming belligerent, nasty and profane. It is only a phone, you crazy, phone-obsessed people!

To close the chapter, let's discuss movie theaters. In a nutshell, you should never, ever have your phone turned on inside a movie theater. The only exception to this civility rule is if you are a doctor or if you have a babysitter at home with the children. If you do fall into one of these two categories, the phone should be on vibrate only. If people are paying an average of $12 bucks each for a ticket plus food and beverage, they do not want to hear your phone ringing, text alerts, app notifications, and never mind someone talking on a phone.

Also, if it is date night, do not go the movies at all. Go to a restaurant, sit on a park bench, splurge on some ice cream or go have a few adult beverages and talk to each other. Please!

SHOOTINGS, RIOTS AND ARRESTS

The next time you watch video footage online or on television of a shooting, a riot, or an arrest, look at what the bystanders are doing. What do the vast majority of them have in common?

Almost all of the onlookers are recording the event or confrontation on their phones. Why is that so many people's first inclination? Wouldn't it be smarter, never mind safer, to get the heck out of the area? Think about it; you have people pushing and shoving, fists flying, cops hitting people over the head with their batons and potentially bullets flying, and your first instinct is to get out your phone and start recording the melee?

I can only think of a few semi-rational reasons for even *considering* doing this, although none of them makes much sense to yours truly.

The first reason is that people want to post their "newsworthy, spectacular and macabre" video online. Well, guess what Einstein! If you are at a riot or a shooting, you may have an issue posting something online. The simple reason is that you may be trampled on by the mob, you may have a bullet in your leg or shoulder, and worst yet, you may be dead because you were dumb enough to stick around and film the so-called newsworthy event. Please, if you happen to be in a dangerous area, hit the road as soon as your legs will carry you far, far away.

Another reason folks may want to record a shooting, riot or an arrest is to go home and share the recording in person with family, friends, or co-workers. Do you think their reaction is going to be: "Oh, how exciting you were there." or "Wow, that must have been an experience of a lifetime." or "I wish you would have called me so I could have gone there as well."?

That is not going to be their reaction at all. They, like any other sane person, is going to think you are either bat shit crazy or a damn fool or both. Enough said.

A third reason people may want to video a shooting, riot or arrest is that their recording can potentially "stick it to the man or stick it to the cops" or someone else in authority. The problem with that thought is that 95 percent of the time you have a video of a cop hitting some drunk ass goofball or robbery suspect but you do not see what happened prior to the arrest or punches being thrown. Cops do not just walk up to people and bash them in the head for no reason. Ninety-nine percent of the time, the perpetrator tried to grab the cop's gun, spit on them or did some other crazy shit. Please do not try to be a social justice warrior with your phone because you hardly ever get to see what led up to the issue in the first place.

The last semi-rational reason I can think of for why people stick around dangerous situations and film, is that they think they can sell their video to the local television station or, better yet, to a national news program or TMZ. Guess what people: the odds of that happening are one in 5 million videos. One in 50 million? One in 100 million? The bottom line is that you have ZERO chance of becoming the next Abraham Zapruder.

For those of you who are under the age of 60, let me digress and explain who Abraham Zapruder was.

Mr. Abraham Zapruder filmed probably the most famous personal video of all time. He took his Bell & Howell 8-millimeter home movie color camera to see President John F. Kennedy and his motorcade come through Dallas on November 22, 1963. Abraham Zapruder positioned himself high on an embankment downtown at Dealey Plaza to get some great angled views and film of the President's motorcade. His video captured the horrendous moment when President Kennedy was shot in the head and shoulder on that fateful day. His film was the primary recording that was used by the Secret Service and the Warren Commission that investigated the assassination. Mr. Zapruder also sold a copy of the film to Life Magazine for $150,000 ($1.5 million in today's dollars) much to the chagrin of the underbidder, CBS News.

Back to the topic at hand: *This is never going to be you!*

So, please walk away from dangerous situations and run away from riots and especially shootings for goodness' sake. Do not get your video phone out. Do not try to be a hero. Do not try to be famous. Take care of yourself instead.

FACETIME

FaceTime is a marvelous invention! It improves a simple phone call, never mind a text message, by a country mile. This terrific visual and voice technology is a wonderful way to share special moments with family, friends and classmates. A few excellent examples include:

- You can share your baby's first steps with your parents, grandparents or even great-grandparents.
- You can FaceTime your parents on their birthdays, or have a video call with your siblings for their birthdays.
- You can check in with your kids while they are away on vacation (are they still looking halfway alive?) or at college (to see if they have put on the freshman fifteen-to-twenty pounds yet).
- You can FaceTime your besties on their own special moments that you cannot physically attend.
- You can have a great visual call for Mother's Day, Father's Day, Christmas and any other holiday that you might celebrate.

But …

For the love of God do it at home and not in a public place!

I have seen and heard hundreds of FaceTime calls in the past five years in public places.

The key question is why? Don't these people realize that:

- They are having a very loud private conversation in a public place?
- No one around them wants to hear this said private conversation?
- That they are being incredibly annoying and downright rude to those around them?

A few years ago, Ann and I were in Miami having breakfast at a local cafe off of South Beach. It was a small restaurant with tables jammed in right next to each other. We ordered food and started chatting about the wild night we had the previous evening when in walks a couple who sit down at the table three-to-four feet away from us. The dude, who was about thirty to thirty-five years old, whipped out his phone and started a really loud FaceTime call with his Mom. The topic of their conversation was not important like his/her health or his/her safety; it was a conversation about total miscellaneous day-to-day crap.

Of course, I asked him politely to take the call outside since Ann and I could not hear each other while conversing. Well, you would have thought I asked this guy for his kidney. He throws a huge hissy fit and gets even louder. Meanwhile, the dude's date or wife or friend is bored out of her mind and has tried to order food but he is too distracted and interested in his call to even look at the menu. The bottom line to this silliness was that the restaurant manager finally told him to shut the phone off or go outside and that finally did the trick. But it again begs the question, why does someone feel that this is okay to do in a public restaurant?

On a recent plane trip from Dallas to Chicago, a kid about twenty years old was sitting a few rows behind me on a FaceTime call with his Dad. At this time, boarding was complete and we were ready to push back from the gate so phones were supposed to be turned off or switched to airplane mode. At this point, the flight attendant (FA) has made the announcement to that effect at least two to three times. But no, this kid is still on the very loud FaceTime call with his Dad. Of course, the FA asks him for the second time to shut the phone down. This is the best part: the father, who is not even on the plane, tells the FA that he wants to make sure the flight takes off okay. WTH?

Since I cannot resist my urges sometimes, I yell back to the kid "Tell your helicopter Dad to get on flightaware.com and punch in the flight number and he can track the flight on the ground, the takeoff and the next two hours of flight time to Chicago". I was not going to let these two dumbasses make 200 other souls on the plane late because he would not get off his damn phone. Mission accomplished!

Finally, as I mentioned in a previous chapter, I volunteer at Dallas Fort Worth International Airport at the Information Desk a few times a month. Last week while on duty, a Hispanic woman was trying to figure out where her connecting gate was so that she could get to Tulsa (she originated in Panama). While she is asking me in Spanish (which thankfully I am fluent in) about her connection, I notice she is on a FaceTime call with some guy who turns out to be her brother.

Every time I went to give her directions going from Terminal D to Terminal E, I was interrupted by her FaceTime brother who is 1,975 miles away in Panama City. After the third time I tried to show/her tell/her how to get to other terminal and her departure gate and was interrupted by the FaceTime brother I said "NO MAS".

At the end of the day, I told her that I would personally escort her to the other terminal on the train and walk her to her gate but only if she terminated this FaceTime call with her brother. Which is exactly what happened. But damn her brother trying to help; he has never been to DFW and he keeps telling her what to do from thousands of miles away!

So, people, use FaceTime all you want because it is an awesome medium to connect with loved ones and friends, but please do not FaceTime in any public places like restaurants, gyms, bars, airports, airplanes, and certainly not in a bloody movie theater.

BATHROOMS

I cannot believe I am going to write a chapter (albeit a short one) on using phones whilst in the bathroom! Unfortunately, I am somewhat forced to since so many people use phones in restrooms.

As mentioned previously, I am a frequent traveler, I eat out quite often, and I am in public places all the time. For this reason (and because I am old), I have to "use the facilities" frequently.

Not to get graphic, but I cannot begin to tell you how many times I have been in the men's restroom and some guy is using the urinal while talking on his phone. What the heck is so damn urgent or necessary?

First, it is rather disgusting and never mind how unsanitary it is. To make matters worse, most of those guys leave the bathroom without washing their hands or sanitizing their phones. YIKES!

Second, more bizarre, are the guys on the throne talking away with someone while "doing their business" and then not washing up after. Double disgusting!

Third, and the worst behavior I have seen, is when people are on a FaceTime call while using the facilities. If the idiot in the bathroom is that rude to not end the call prior to going to the restroom, then why doesn't the party on the other end get grossed out and end the call? Can you imagine being on the other end of that FaceTime call? Triple disgusting and big-time rude.

That is what I have personally seen hundreds of times in the past five years or more. People talking and FaceTiming in restrooms at restaurants, airports, bars and theaters.

Since I am a dude, I do not know what happens in the ladies' restrooms. I did have a conversation on this topic with my fabulous girlfriend Ann and my fantastic daughter Meg. In a nutshell, they told me that women are actually equally disgusting about using their phones in restrooms in public places. My awesome niece and Goddaughter Ellie (who provided excellent feedback on this manuscript as I was writing it) also mentioned to me that "women have a tendency to make TikTok videos in public restrooms and post them while there are others around them who are trying to take care of their business in peace" DOUBLE YIKES!

So, please people, stay off your phones while in public bathrooms and in your private bathrooms, too.

CONCLUSION

As discussed at the beginning of this book, smartphones, laptops, desktop computers, tablets and gaming consoles are ubiquitous. There are almost seven *billion* smartphones alone in use today across the globe.

As I mentioned numerous times, smartphones are one of the biggest, if not one of the most successful, inventions since electricity was created. The smartphone allows us to be exceptionally efficient and productive.

As an example of the productivity and efficiency smartphones have (for those of you old enough to remember), think back twenty or more years ago and remember what it took to plan and execute a summer family vacation. Back in those days, you would have to:

- Look through endless hard copies of brochures to decide where you wanted to go.
- Visit a travel agency to discuss the trip and begin to plan flights, hotels, rental cars and other details.
- Make countless phone calls from your landline phone to explore and book excursions or tours and other vacation-type reservations.

- Return to the travel agency to finalize the trip and get your physical airline tickets and, in some cases, paper hotel vouchers.

Think about today, where you can plan and finalize the location, flights, hotels, car rentals, restaurants and/or excursion tickets for a trip in about thirty to sixty minutes using your smartphone. This is extremely efficient, to say the least.

However, the use of and obsession with smartphones has gotten incredibly out of control. When the average American currently spends five hours a day, and is projected to spend almost 110,000 hours– or 21 % of their lifetime on their devices, it is definitely time to rethink how we spend our collective time.

Recently we spent two weeks in Western Europe, and I can tell you that people there seem to be on their phones even more than five hours a day. Incredible !

If people were only connecting with family and friends or just checking emails while using their smartphones, that would make sense and be perfectly nice and normal. However, where most people spend time while on their devices is on highly addictive social media platforms.

It is very concerning that on average Facebook users spend sixty-four minutes a day on their site and Instagram users spend forty-eight minutes per day on that site. It is no wonder that survey after survey shows that people are more tired, distracted, lonely and depressed than ever before. Furthermore, phone obsession has clearly led to most people having little to no basic social skills.

If you do not believe me, wait until I tell you about a recent study conducted in 2023 that I discovered while writing this short book.

Apparently, there is a *World Happiness Report* that is conducted every few years. Who knew, right?

According to this worldwide survey, the United States ranked 23rd overall on the happiness score; the first time it had dropped out of the top 20 since the first survey was conducted in 2002. (If you are interested in the top results, the Nordic countries were all in the top four worldwide).

The detailed survey data shows that adults over the age of sixty in the United States were the 10th happiest worldwide, which is awesome. Good for us old farts!

However, young people under the age of thirty in the United States ranked 62nd out of 143 countries. Trust me, many of the 143 countries participating are not places you would ever want to visit; never mind live there.

Then why the very poor ranking in this survey for those younger than thirty years old in the United States? According to the University of Oxford researchers, "the findings are concerning because youth well-being and mental health is highly predictive of a whole host of subjective and objective indicators of quality of life as people age and go through the course of life".

The researchers went on to add "youth in the United States now start lower than adults in terms of well-being. And that's very disconcerting because essentially it means that they're at the level of their mid-life crisis today".

Finally, regarding this survey, researchers added that in the United States, they spoke to Kindergarten through Grade 12 students who mentioned "talking about a change in culture where there's no longer a culture of speaking to each other. And that's really horrible because we all know from well-being science that nothing's more important than your social capital -- having quality connections and people to rely on and speak with on a very frequent basis".

Wow, how scary is the fact that our youth are so unhappy? In addition, being ranked 23rd across all ages overall is not something we should be proud of.

Therefore, to test a theory, I ask you to consider this:

Imagine if you won a raffle that gave you the use of a two-to-three-bedroom beachfront home for the entire summer that was only a two-to-three-hour drive away from where you live. Now say theoretically you would like to have friends come visit you every weekend for the duration of the summer.

Make a mental or written list right now of the people you would want to invite.

How many couples/friends would be on that list that you are willing to share a weekend with at your (free) summer home? Do you have enough people to invite to fill in all eight-to-ten weekends? Do you have enough people to fill in half?

If the answer is filling in less than half, then we need to start making more friends but, most importantly, deeper, more meaningful and fun friendships and relationships with those around us.

Think about the phone obsession this way: when you finally put your phone down after playing with it for quite a while, did you learn anything new or meaningful? Did you just scroll and scroll aimlessly because it is such a bad habit at this point? (Thanks Ellie!)

From the data I shared, it is apparent that we all need to get off our phones and laptops, minimize the social media addiction, and start building meaningful connections with real, live human beings.

I sincerely hope that I have pointed out ten to twelve locations and circumstances where we can and should put down our phones and start engaging with those around us.

Having meaningful and quality friendships will not solve all of your happiness issues, but it will certainly make you feel more *CONNECTED,* more *ENGAGED* and more *LOVED.*

SO, PLEASE LIVE EVERY DAY LIKE IT IS YOUR LAST DAY INTERACTING WITH PEOPLE!

(Please read the next page ... thank you.)

I NEED A FAVOR —PLEASE

If you enjoyed reading this book, or even mildly enjoyed it, I was wondering if you could do me a big favor ...

... and try to help me increase the circulation of this book.

Specifically, I am asking you to please buy another copy of this book.

That way you would have this copy and a new one in your midst to pass along to two of your friends or family members. Then in time the two people you gave your two books to would then pass along four books to others and they in turn will pass along eight books and that way we can get the number of people reading this this book up dramatically over time.

The cost of the book is very inexpensive on Amazon and other places where you purchase books online. In fact the cost is:

- about the same as a Big Mac meal at McDonald's or
- roughly the cost of one beer at a nice bar or restaurant or
- approximately half the price of a glass of wine while you are out or
- half of the cost for a one month's subscription to Netflix.

SO, A VERY SINCERE THANK YOU IN ADVANCE FOR HELPING SPREAD THE WORD.

ACKNOWLEDGMENTS

The old adage that you never write a book alone is certainly very true. I could have never completed this book, never mind getting it published, if it was not for the tremendous help of so many people.

First of all to Ann, who not only gave me the encouragement to sit down and write but bought me a boatload of books, pamphlets and "how to" guides on writing. It was immensely helpful, and I am forever grateful.

To those who were my "beta readers", who perused through the very early version of my manuscript and provided fantastic feedback: Helen, Ellie, Cindi, Nick, Chris, Anthony, Kevin, Cathy, Rachael, Erin, Harrison and, of course, Meg and Ann; a sincere THANK YOU. Your commentary and point of view on both big points and small ones was hugely helpful.

A special thanks to Ellie, Helen, Cathy and Meg for providing a very detailed written review on what you liked and did not like and gave me very specific feedback on the entire manuscript. I cannot thank the four of you enough.

Finally, a huge thanks to Mary O' and Helen who edited this book for me. The kid (me) who grew up in Puerto Rico obviously did not spend a lot of time studying the English language and most especially the grammar lessons at school. Hence Mary and Helen had their work cut out for them and did an awesome job.

So, leave your phone at home and go out, engage with people and enjoy life ~

NOTES
AND REFERENCES

Chapter 1: Phone Ubiquity and Apps
Dallas Morning News 12/13/23 via the Associated Press "1 in 6 teens say use "almost constant"

Chapter 1: Phone Ubiquity and Apps
Dallas Morning News 11/27/23 Author : Louis A. Bedford IV "Is it Social media or are we awkward and alone?"

Chapter 7: Driving
National Highway Traffic Safety Administration. NHTSA.Gov Distracted Driving Statistics

Chapter 12: Conclusion
Dallas Morning News 3/24/24. "America's Happiness Scores Takes Hit From Youth Crisis"
By Victoria Bassett, The Washington Post
Jan - Emmanuel De Neve, Director of the University of Oxford's Well Being Research Center.

BIOGRAPHY

Tom Reynolds is a first-time author.

As a child and as an adult, he has lived in five different countries and has made his home in eleven different cities (so far).

A former Sales and Marketing Executive with the Quaker Oats Company, The Gatorade Company, and PepsiCo, Inc., he has enjoyed thousands of personal relationships and engagements in his thirty-five-year career.

He has become a keen observer of the recent lack of social interaction and social skill development in society given the advent and obsession with smartphone use.

Tom resides in Dallas, Texas.

He can be reached on X/Twitter by @reynolds_tom